MAKING FANTASTIC ALIENS AND SPACESHIPS

This edition produced in **1993** for
Shooting Star Press Inc
230 Fifth Avenue
New York, NY 10001

Design David West
Children's Book Design
Designer Keith Newell
Editor Michael Flaherty
Photography Roger Vlitos

Created and produced by
Aladdin Books Ltd
28 Percy Street
London W1P 9FF

First published in
the United States in 1992 by
Gloucester Press

ISBN 1-56924-031-0

Printed in Belgium

Why throw it away?

MAKING FANTASTIC ALIENS AND SPACESHIPS

SHOOTING STAR PRESS

JEN GREEN

Contents

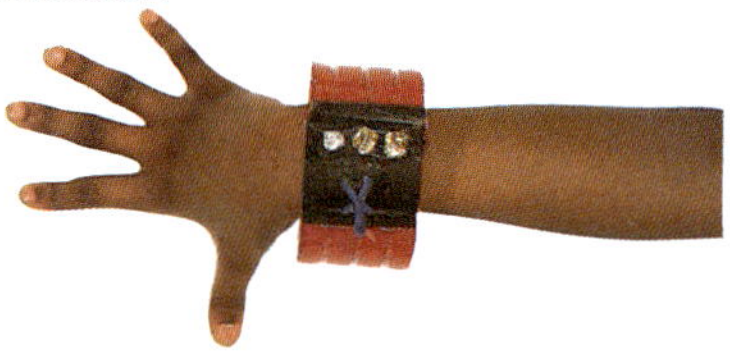

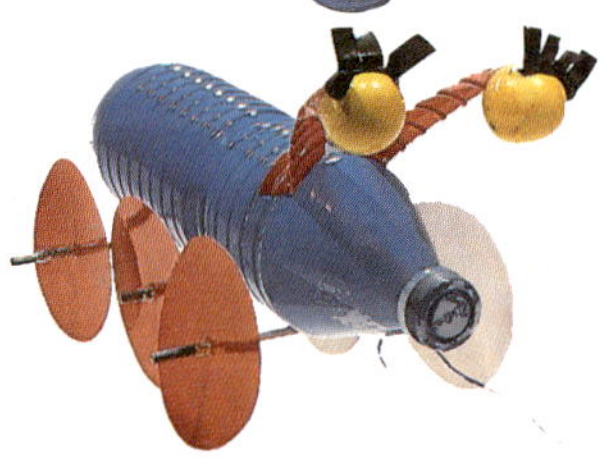

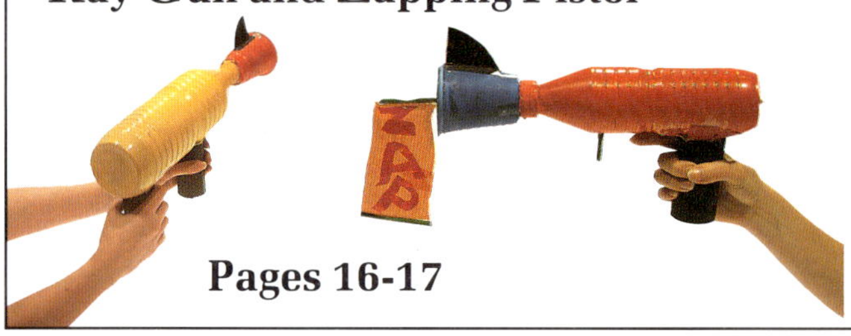

Introduction

This book will show you how to make your own collection of fantastic aliens and spaceships – toys and action models that race or fly. Each project is explained in easy stages. There are also ideas about how you can decorate the models, bringing in your own imagination.

New for old

All the models described in this book can be made from everyday junk that you and your family usually throw away. Each project provides a list of junk items that can be used to make the model. But if you haven't got one of the items suggested, don't worry; you may have something that will do just as well.

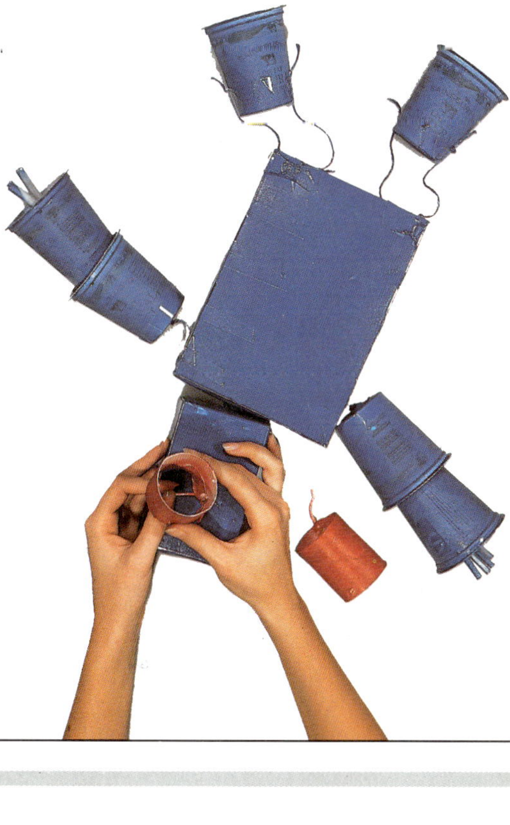

Collecting junk

Start your collection of junk materials now. Save anything that might come in handy, and ask your family to pass junk to you rather than throw it away. Make sure your materials are clean before you store them, in plastic bags or in a big cardboard box.

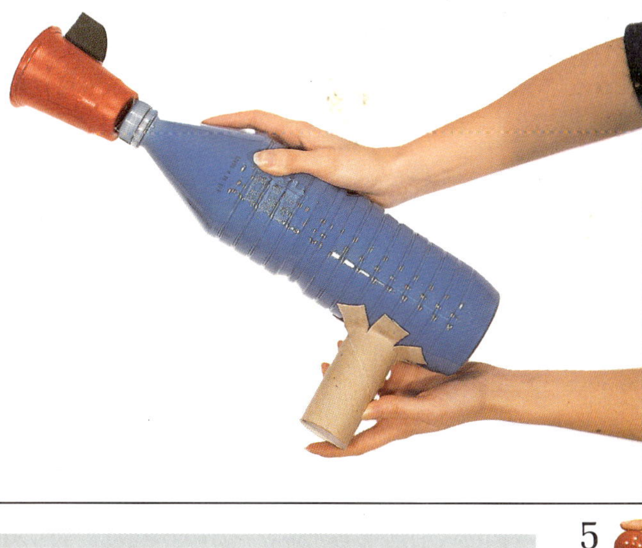

Balloon-powered Rocket

This simple rocket, driven by a balloon, streaks through space when its balloon is released. The rocket zooms along a string tied between two pieces of furniture.

Step By Step

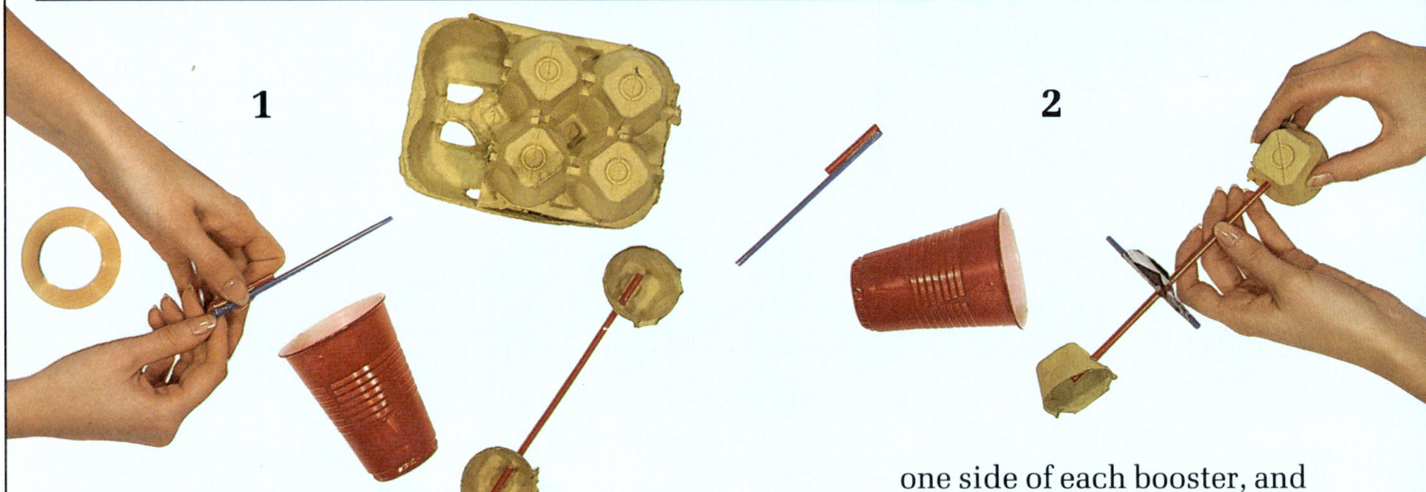

1 The rocket runs on a string through guides attached to the nose and tail of the model. To make the guide for the nose, cut a short piece of drinking straw and attach it to a long straw with tape. The guide for the tail will be attached to two rocket boosters which are made with two egg cartoon segments. Pierce a hole in one side of each booster, and thread them onto another straw. Secure the boosters in position with tape.

2 Cut another short piece of straw for the tail guide. Attach it at right-angles to the boosters' straw with

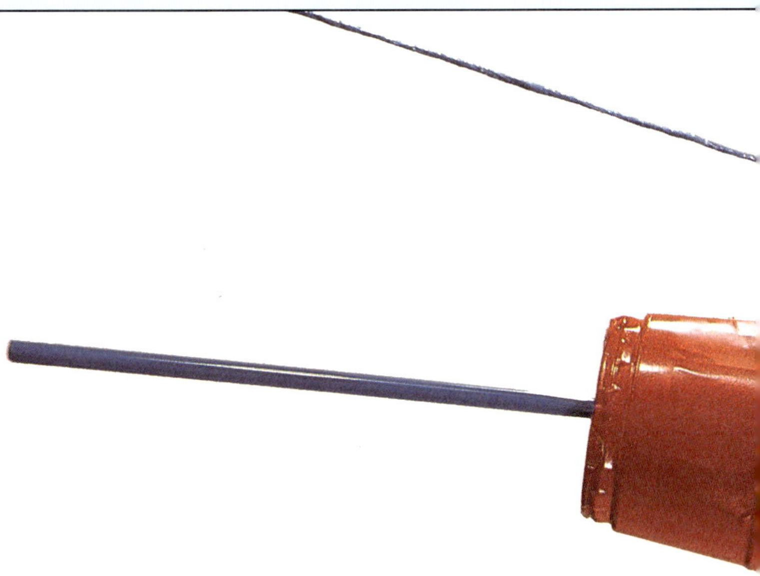

Your rocket runs along a string anchored between two pieces of furniture. Tie one end of a long piece of string to one anchor point. Thread the other end through the straws on the nose and tail of the rocket. Stretch the string taut and tie it to your second anchor point.

YOU CAN USE:

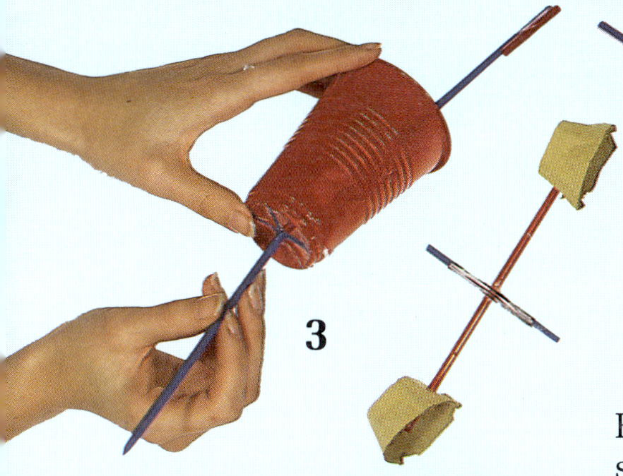

3

4

tape. Cut a cardboard fin for the tail guide and stick it on the tail guide.
3 The rocket's nose is made with a clean plastic cup. Tape the long straw attached to the nose guide to the inside of the cup as shown.

For the nose probe, cut a series of slits into the end of another straw (see Practical Tips on page 28). Splay the cut ends of the straw flat on the bottom of the cup and tape them down. **4** Blow up the balloon. Tape its neck up tightly to prevent air from escaping. Tape the nose and tail to the balloon, to complete your rocket.

Release the neck of the balloon and watch your rocket jet off along the string!

Wrist Communicator

No sounds can travel through space, but you can keep in touch with fellow astronauts or with base control with the help of this radio communicator.

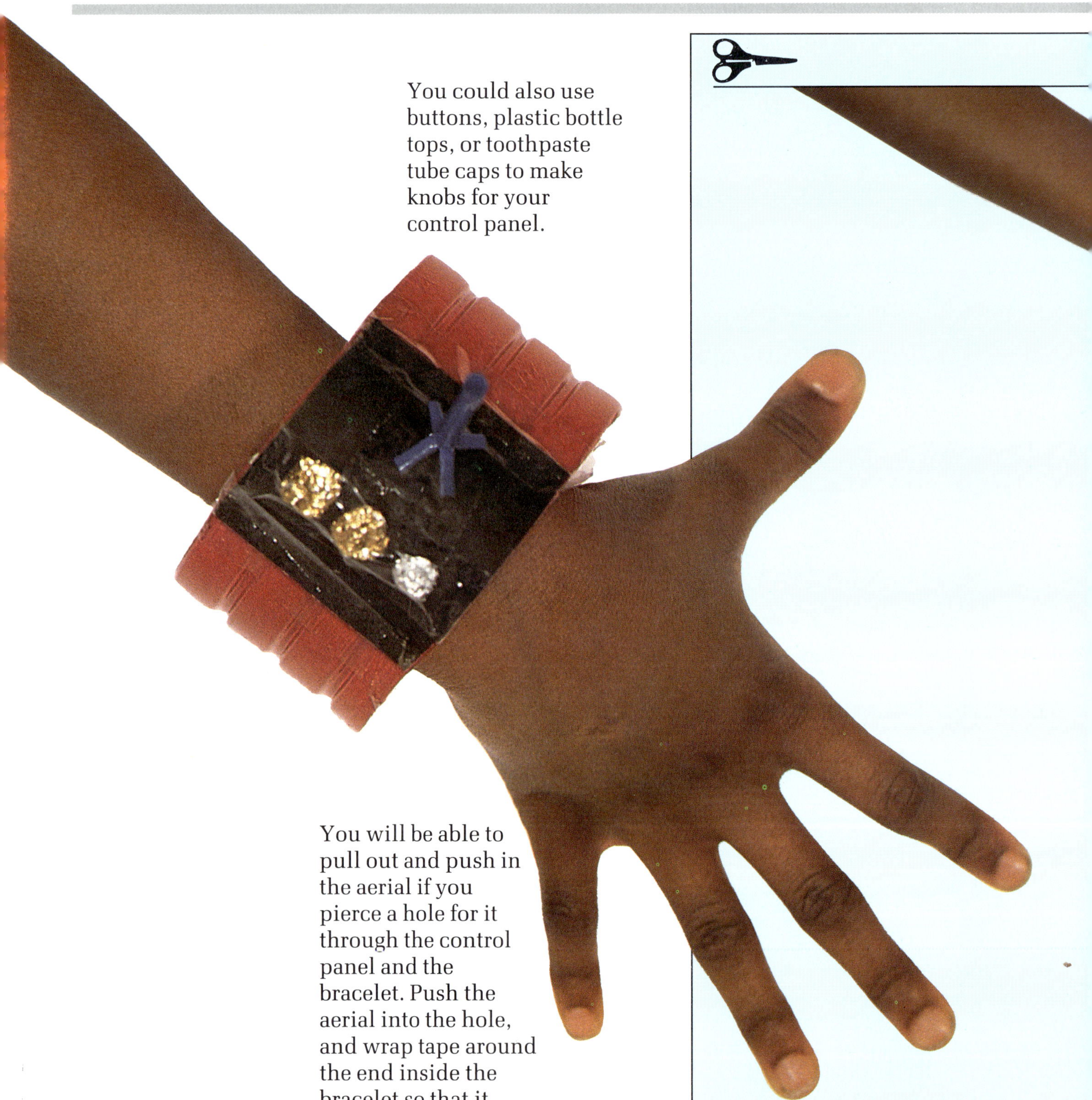

You could also use buttons, plastic bottle tops, or toothpaste tube caps to make knobs for your control panel.

You will be able to pull out and push in the aerial if you pierce a hole for it through the control panel and the bracelet. Push the aerial into the hole, and wrap tape around the end inside the bracelet so that it does not fall out.

1 Cut the bracelet from the middle section of a plastic bottle. To make the bracelet

YOU CAN USE:

STEP BY STEP

1

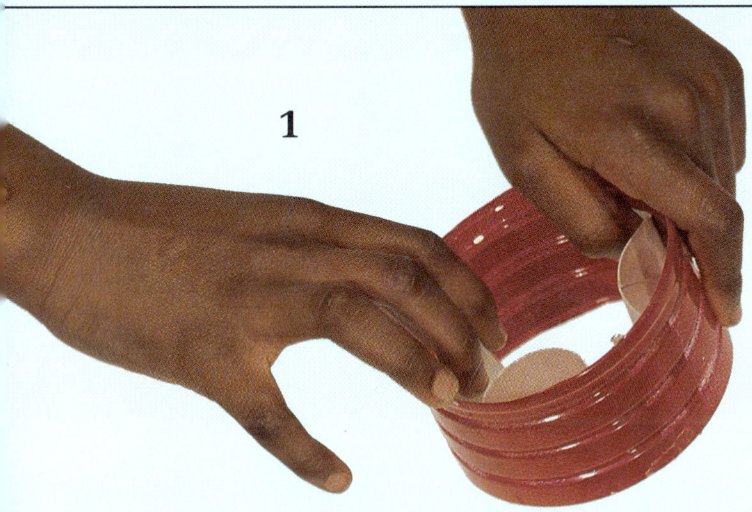

2

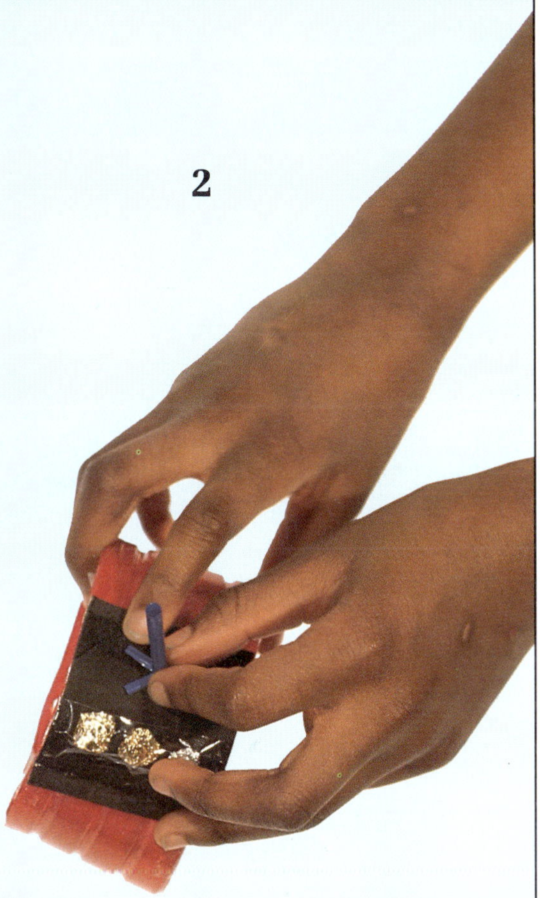

fit your wrist, you will need adjusters, made from a toilet paper tube. With scissors, cut the tube in half lengthwise and then widthwise, to form four sections. Fold the edges of the sections back to make flaps. Tape the flaps around the inside of the bracelet. Try the bracelet on and add or take away adjusters until it fits. **2** The control panel of the communicator is made with a quarter section cut from another toilet paper tube. Fold the edges back to make flaps and tape it to the outside of the bracelet. Now make buttons for the control panel from tinfoil. Roll small pieces of foil into tiny balls and then flatten them between your fingers. Glue or tape them to the panel. Make an antenna for your radio communicator with a drinking straw. Cut a series of slits into one end of the straw. Splay the cut ends of the straw flat onto the panel and tape them down.

Alien Feet

These wacky alien feet are a must for space games and fancy dress parties. The ones shown here have long, crinkly veins and brightly colored toes.

Step By Step

1 Make two alien feet by cutting a cardboard tissue box in half. If you haven't got a tissue box, any flat cardboard box will do. Cut segments from an egg carton for toes – you could have ten, or more if you choose! Cut four long strips of cardboard to make veins. Crease the cardboard into accordion folds as shown. **2** Glue or tape the toes and veins to the feet. The alien species shown here has two toes on the top of each foot, and veins running down the top and side. To fit the feet around your own, you will need to make two heels. To make one of these, cut two strips of cardboard. Pierce a hole near the end of each strip. Link the two strips with a piece of string about 20 inches long. Thread the ends of the string through the holes and knot the ends. Repeat this to make a second heel. **3** Tape the strips inside the feet as shown.

YOU CAN USE:

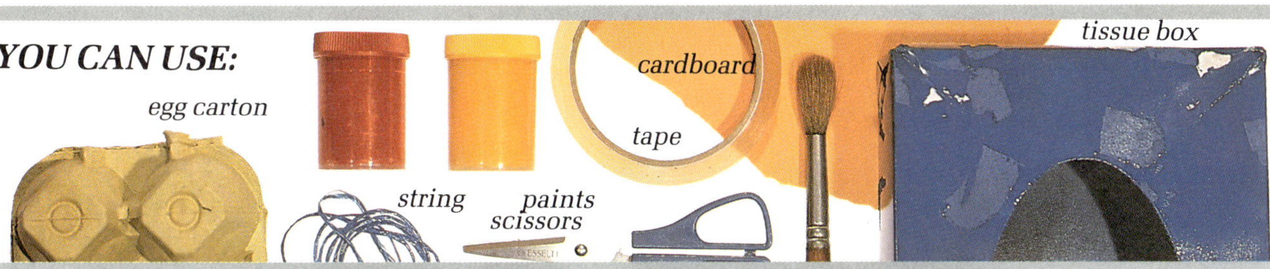

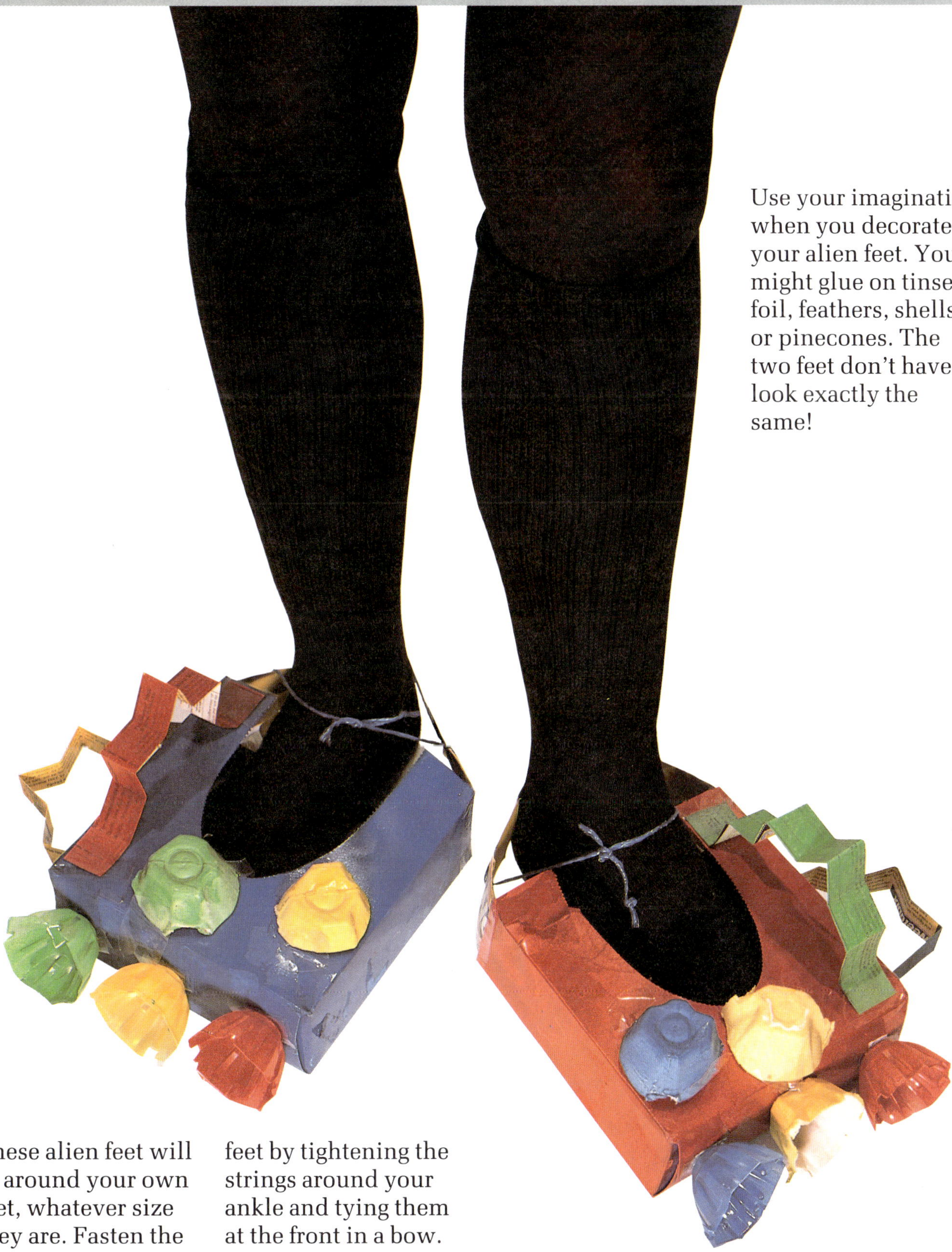

Use your imagination when you decorate your alien feet. You might glue on tinsel, foil, feathers, shells, or pinecones. The two feet don't have to look exactly the same!

These alien feet will fit around your own feet, whatever size they are. Fasten the feet by tightening the strings around your ankle and tying them at the front in a bow.

Reggie The Robot

Reggie is a young robot and his movements can be shy and clumsy. You can control him by using the handle attached to his back.

Step By Step

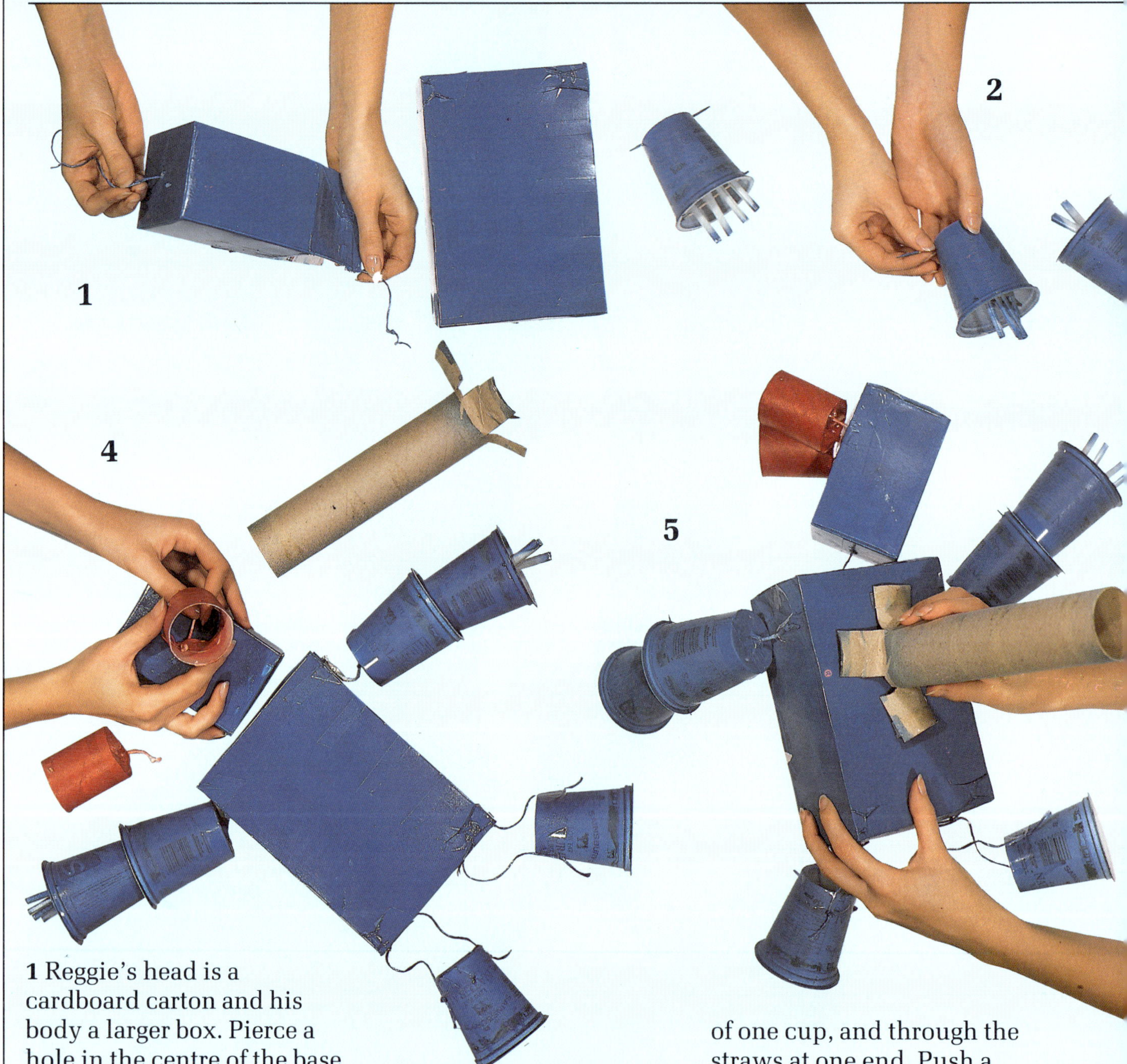

1 Reggie's head is a cardboard carton and his body a larger box. Pierce a hole in the centre of the base of the carton. Thread through a short piece of string. Tape up the carton. Tape the string to the top of the box. **2** The arms are made of two plastic cups each, and the fingers are four drinking straw pieces. To attach fingers, pierce holes on opposite sides of the top of one cup, and through the straws at one end. Push a toothpick through one of the holes in the cup. Thread on the fingers and then push it through the other hole.
3 To attach the hand to the

YOU CAN USE:

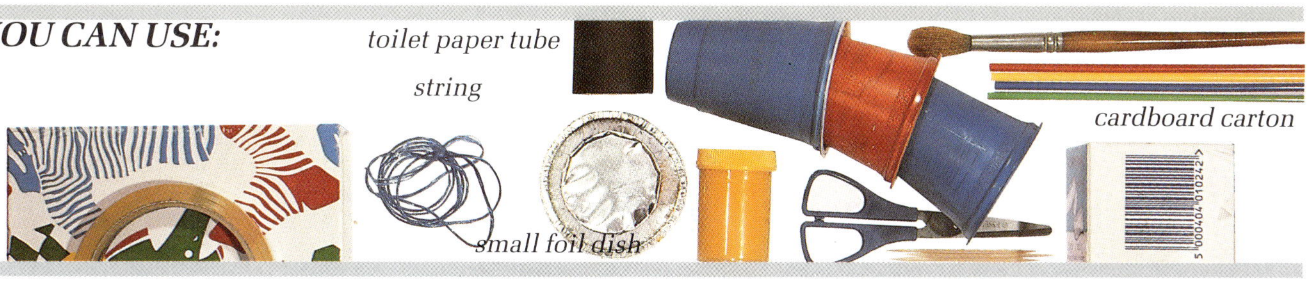

toilet paper tube

string

cardboard carton

small foil dish

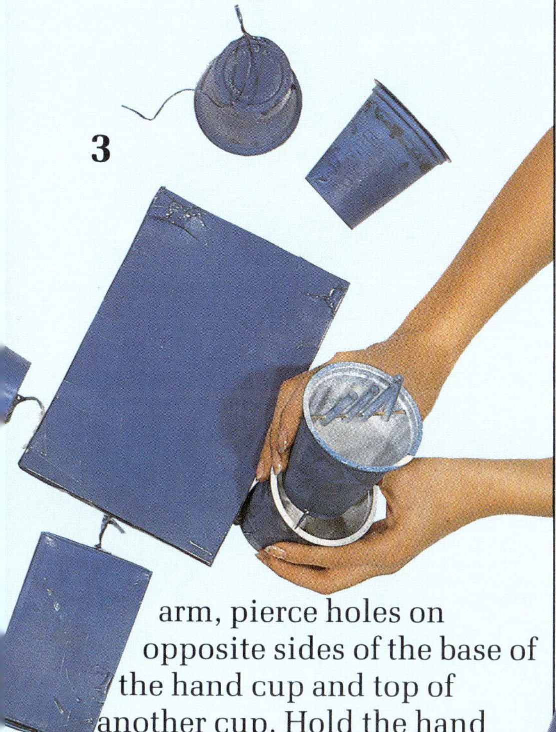

3

arm, pierce holes on opposite sides of the base of the hand cup and top of another cup. Hold the hand cup inside the arm cup, and pass a toothpick through the holes. The hand cup hangs inside the other. To attach an arm to the body, make knots at either end of a piece of string, and tape the string in front of the knots to the arm cup and to the body. **4** Reggie's eyes are made from a toilet paper tube cut in half. Attach them to the head with short pieces of knotted string, as you did the arms. His feet are plastic cups, taped on in the same way. Use longer pieces of string, knotted and taped to both sides of each cup. Now make a control handle for the robot with a paper towel tube. Cut slits in one end to make flaps (see page 28). **5** Splay the flaps against Reggie's back and tape them securely.

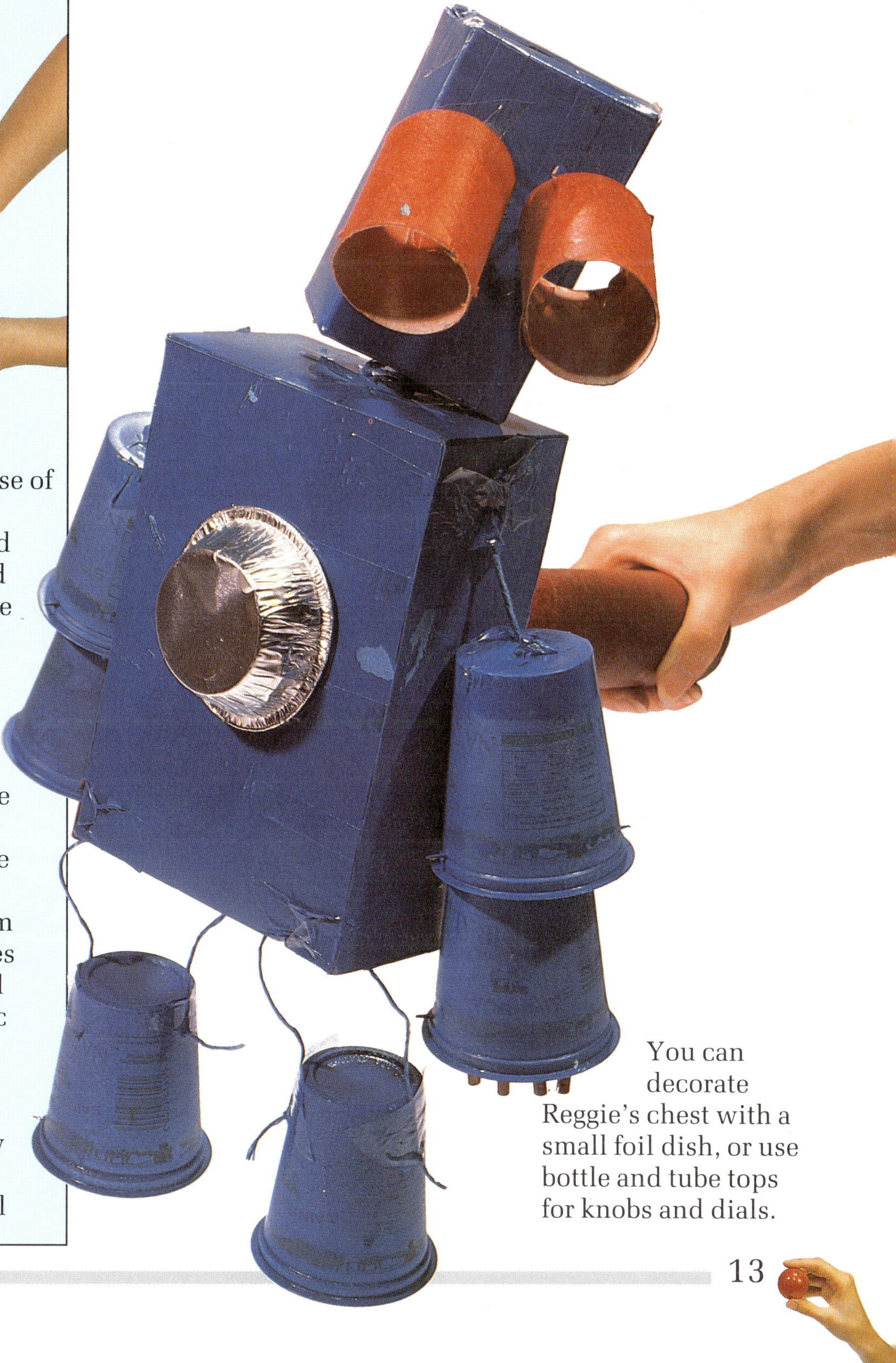

You can decorate Reggie's chest with a small foil dish, or use bottle and tube tops for knobs and dials.

Bug-eyed Monster

This alien species has fearsome eyes that wobble as the monster is pulled along. The model is a fast, smooth runner that can be raced on any flat surface.

Step By Step

1 The monster's body is made from a plastic bottle. Cut long strips from the side of a second bottle for its eye stalks. **2** To make the wheels, draw six cardboard circles by tracing around the bottom of the plastic bottle. Cut them out with scissors. Pierce a hole in the center of each wheel. The wheel cross struts are three short pieces of garden stake. Push one end of each stake through one of the wheels. You could wind tape around the ends outside the wheels to secure them. **3** The stake cross struts are threaded through three short drinking straws taped across the underside of the bottle. Tape the straws in place and thread the canes through the straws (see page 28). Thread the remaining wheels onto the stakes and wind tape around the ends to secure them. **4** The monster's eyes are made from Ping Pong balls. Tape them onto the plastic bottle stalks. For eyelashes, cut two small rectangles from a plastic trash can liner, and fringe them on one side with scissors. Tape on the eyelashes. Crease the other end of the stalks and tape them to the body.

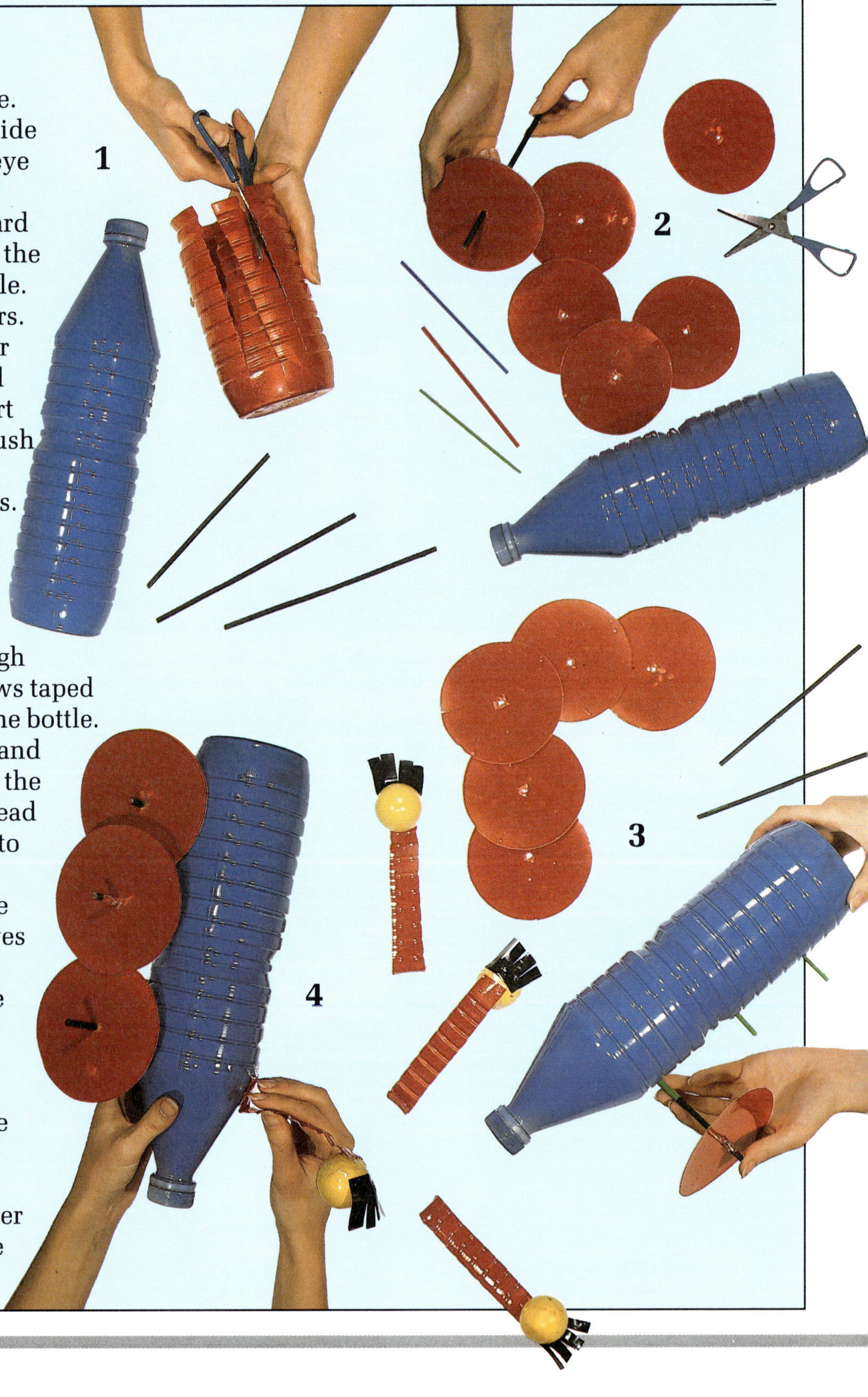

YOU CAN USE:

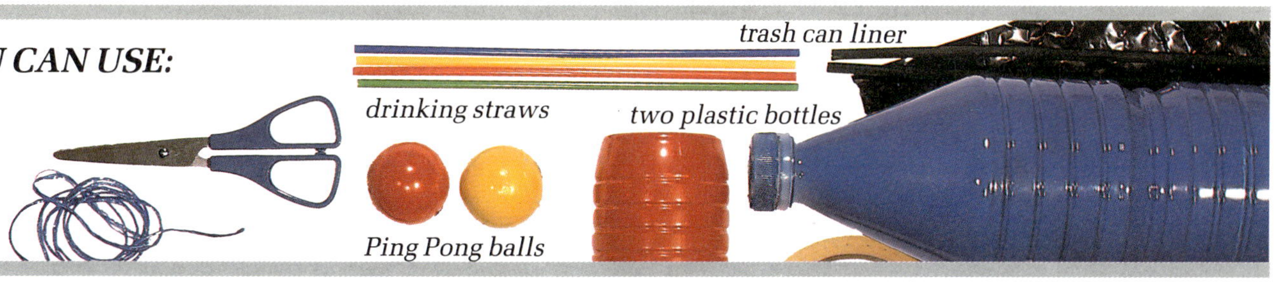

Paint your monster with bright poster colors. You could paint the body with spots or stripes.

You could attach a string to the front of the monster's body to pull it along. Or make two models with a friend, and race them down a smooth, angled surface.

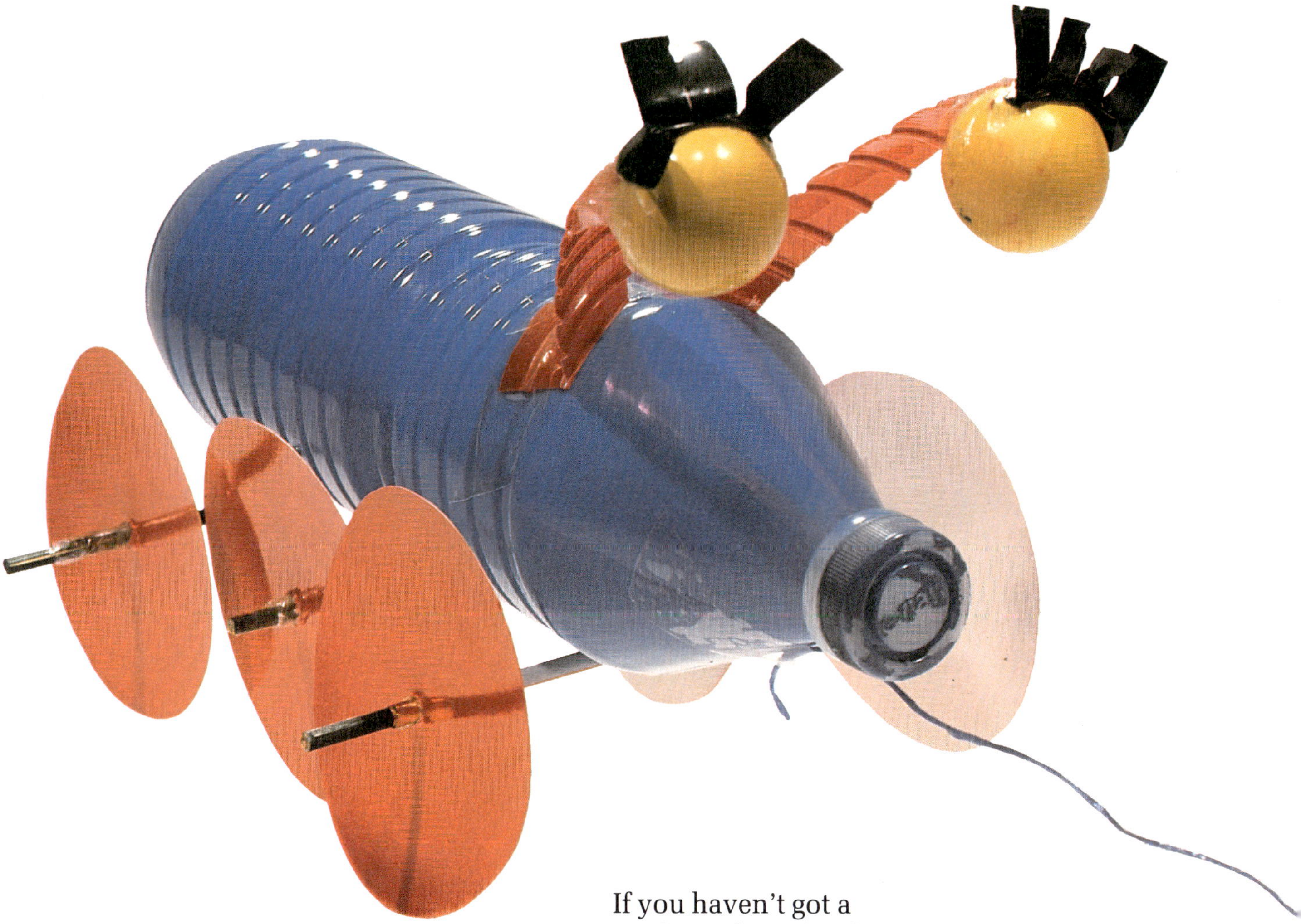

If you haven't got a trash can liner for the eyelashes, you could make them from cardboard or tissue paper instead.

Ray Gun & Zapping Pistol

No star war would be complete without a ray gun or pistol to zap unwary aliens. But beware, the monsters you meet may fight back with weapons of their own!

Step By Step

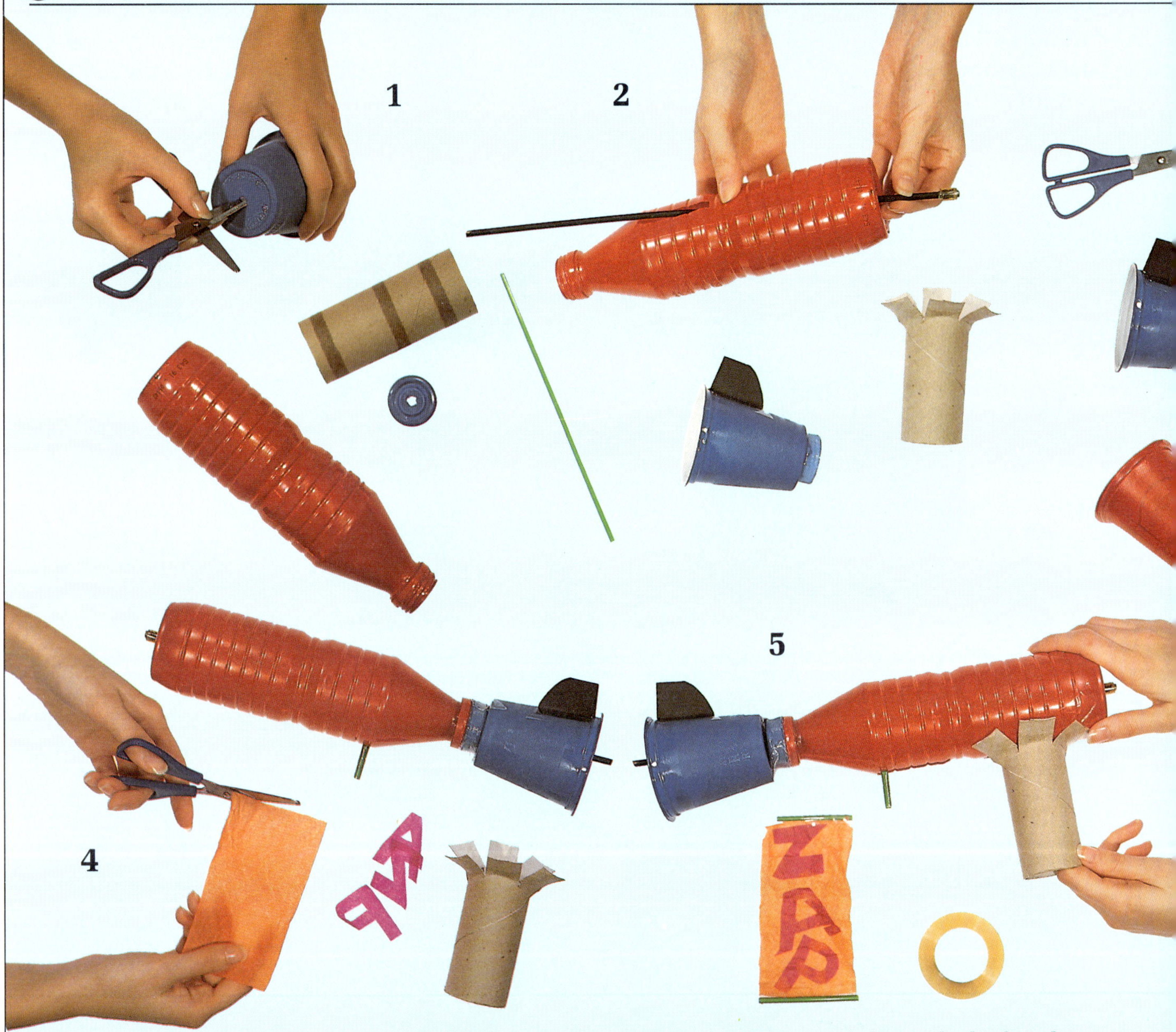

1 For the zapping pistol's barrel and muzzle, pierce a hole through the base of a cup, and through the lid and base of a bottle. **2** For the handle, cut slits into the end of a toilet paper tube. Splay the end flat (see page 28). Cut a fin shape from cardboard and tape it to the muzzle. Cut a trigger slot in the side of the bottle, about 2in long and ½in wide. Wind tape around one end of a garden stake. Push the other end through the bottle's base and the trigger slot. **3** For the trigger, fold a drinking straw in half and tape it around the stake. **4** Push the stake through the neck of the bottle. Thread the bottle top onto the stake and screw it on

YOU CAN USE:

3

6

the bottle. Thread on the cup. For the Zap! flag use a rectangle of paper. Cut the letters from different colored paper and glue them on.

5 Tape pieces of straw to the top and bottom of the flag. Fit the top straw over the end of the stake. Tape the handle onto the pistol.

To load the pistol, pull the trigger back with your finger. To fire it, push the trigger forward. The flag will pop from the muzzle and unfurl to zap your victim.

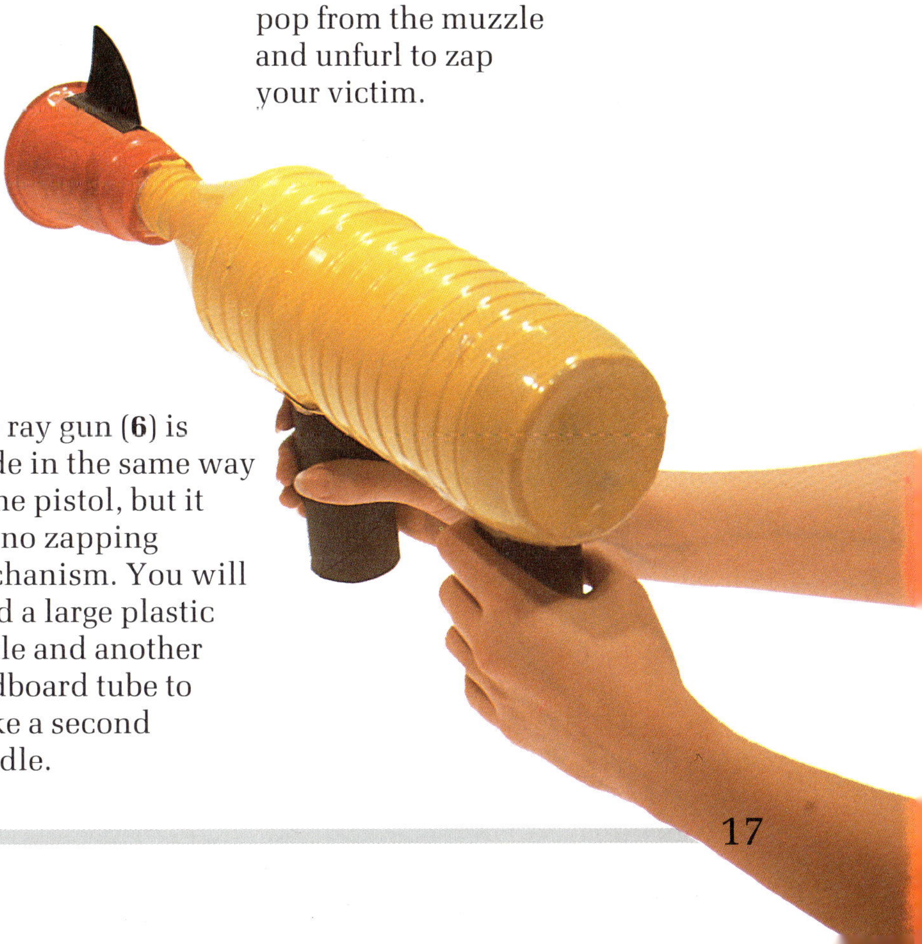

The ray gun (**6**) is made in the same way as the pistol, but it has no zapping mechanism. You will need a large plastic bottle and another cardboard tube to make a second handle.

Space Voyager Mobile

This mobile features an astronaut on a trip around our solar system, and some of the sights he or she might expect to see on the way.

Step By Step

1

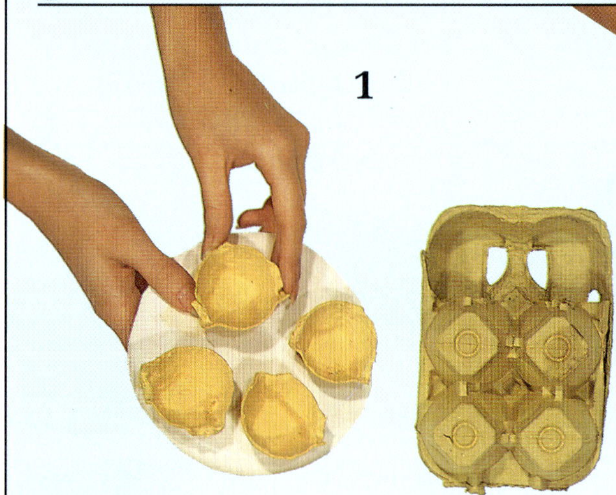

2

4

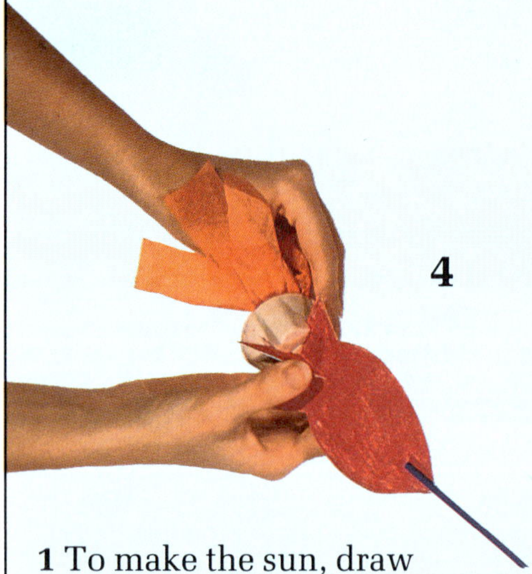

5

1 To make the sun, draw round a circular object on cardboard. Cut out the circle. The sunspots on the sun are egg carton segments. Tape or glue the sunspots onto the sun. **2** The spaceship has a rocket booster, with tissue paper flames. The booster is another egg carton segment. Make a hole in the top of the booster, and push tissue paper strips through. Secure them with tape. **3** Cut out a cardboard shape for the rocket, using the pattern on page 31. Cut out the crossfin, using the pattern on page 30. Cut a slot in the tail to take the crossfin. The probe for the rocket nose is a straw cut down at an angle as shown. Glue or tape on the probe. **4** Cut four slits at right angles to one another on the top of the egg carton booster. Slot the booster onto the tail of the rocket. **5** Use a small ball to make a planet. Cut a strip around a plastic bottle to form the planet's ring. **6** Cut shapes for the crescent moon and star from cardboard, using the patterns on pages 31. Cover them with

YOU CAN USE:

foil of different colors. Use the two patterns on page 30 stuck back to back for the Astronaut. Make a cross-frame by tying two stakes together with string.

Attach the models to the crossframe with thread. Small clay blobs help balance the models.

Attach a large paper clip to the frame so you can hang it somewhere. Attach the frame with thread if you want it to turn freely.

Your mobile could feature Earth, Mars, Venus, or other planets from our solar system.

Crazy Moonbug

This strange species is adapted to travel in the rough craters of the moon. Its off-center wheels make the model wobble crazily when it is pulled along.

Step By Step

1 Make the moonbug's body from a clean plastic dish. Tape a drinking straw across the top of the dish. Push a garden stake through the straw (see page 28). **2** The stake forms a cross strut for the moonbug's back wheels, made from the lids of aerosol cans. Pierce a hole in the top of both lids for the stake to go through. The holes should be placed off-center on each lid, to produce the moonbug's wobbling movement. Cut two small cardboard circles for the front wheels. Make a support for the front wheel with two straws. Join the straws together by taping them in the middle and at one end. Attach the circles to this end by pushing a toothpick through the center

YOU CAN USE:

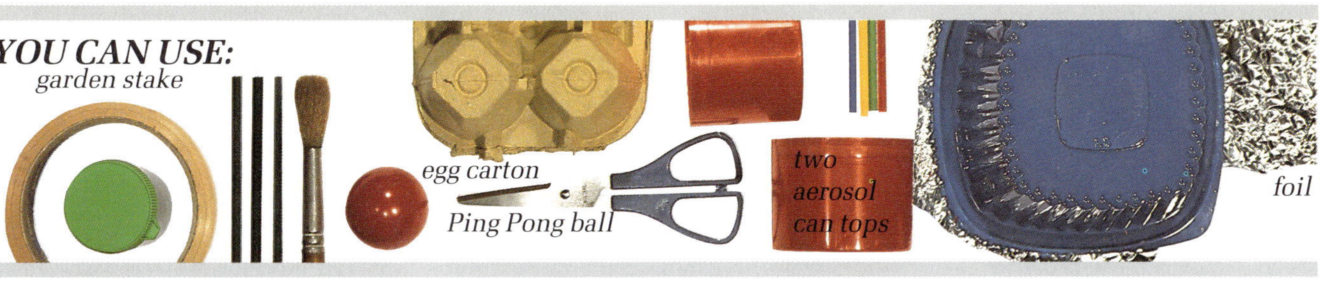

of one circle, through the straws and then through the other circle. Fold the other ends of the straws back to form a T-shape. **3** Tape the T-shape to the front of the moonbug's body. Push the back wheels onto the cross strut. Cut two egg carton segments for eyes and tape them on.

Tape on a Ping Pong or cotton ball for moonbug's nose. Paint pupils in the egg carton eyes.

Cut strips of tinfoil, yarn, or tissue paper to make hair. Tape or glue them to the moonbug's head.

You could also use a large plastic cup for moonbug's body, and segments cut from a chocolate box tray to make the eyes.

Flying Saucer Outfit

This spectacular outfit should provide you with a passport to parties and games on planet Earth and throughout the universe.

Step By Step

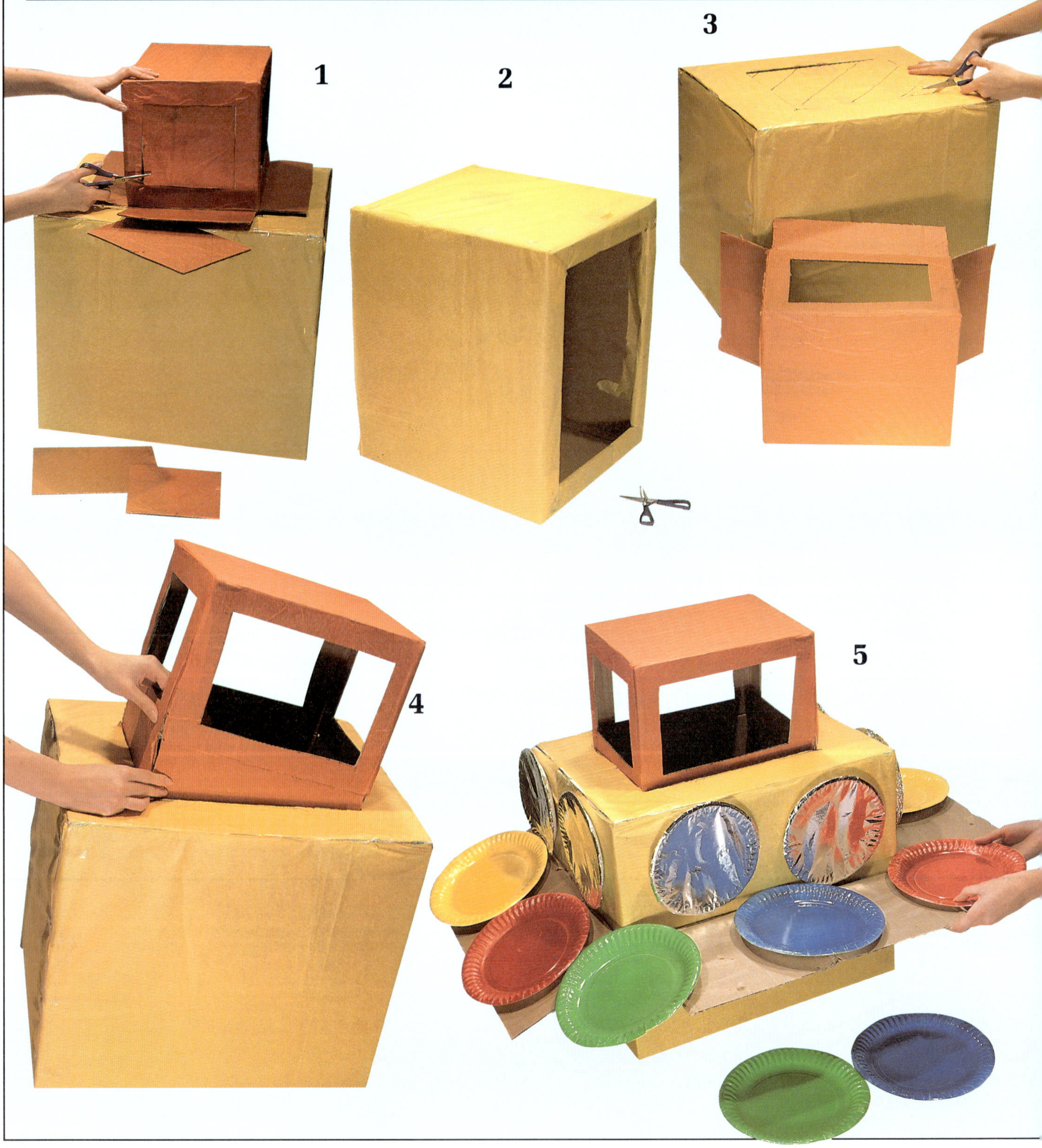

YOU CAN USE:

1 To make the flying saucer outfit you will need a big cardboard box for the body, and a smaller one for the head. Mark a large square inside each of the four sides on the small box. Cut the squares out with scissors. **2** Mark a large square on the bottom of the big box and cut it out. **3** Close the small box and place it on top of the big one. Mark around the small box with a pen and cut out the square that you have drawn on the big box. **4** Open the flaps of the small box and push them through the neck hole you made in the big box.

Tape the flaps of the small box flat inside the top of the big box. **5** Now build the saucer shape around the body, using large flaps of cardboard. Fold the flaps around the body as shown, and tape them on. Tape cardboard struts under the flaps if you want them to stick out. Decorate the saucer shape with cardboard circles or paper plates.

Paint your saucer outfit with bright poster paint. You could wrap tinfoil around some of the cardboard circles on the body. You could also cut armholes in the body if you wish.

You can use a drinking straw to make an antenna for the roof of the saucer. Cut slits in one end of the straw, splay the end flat on the roof, and tape it down.

Powered Space Crawler

This small, menacing creature has a generator driven by a rubber band. Wind up the generator, and watch the alien creep along.

Step By Step

1 Make the crawler's body by cutting two strips of trash can liner (or black paper) about 4 x 3 in. Fringe both strips with scissors. **2** Make the crawler's eyes by cutting a small circle of paper in half. Now begin the creature's generator by cutting a piece of candle about ½ in long. Remove the wick from the piece of candle and enlarge the hole a little. Thread a small rubber band through the hole. You may need to hook it through using a bit of wire or a straightened paper clip. **3** Push a toothpick through the loop at one end of the rubber band to secure it inside the candle. Hook the other end through a cotton spool. **4** Fasten a paper clip onto this end of the rubber band and tape the clip firmly to the side of the spool. Now straighten out two paper clips, and tape one along the top of each of the fringes you made earlier. **5** Make one end of each clip into a hook. Push the hooks into the hole in the candle, so that they sit over the toothpick.

YOU CAN USE:

3

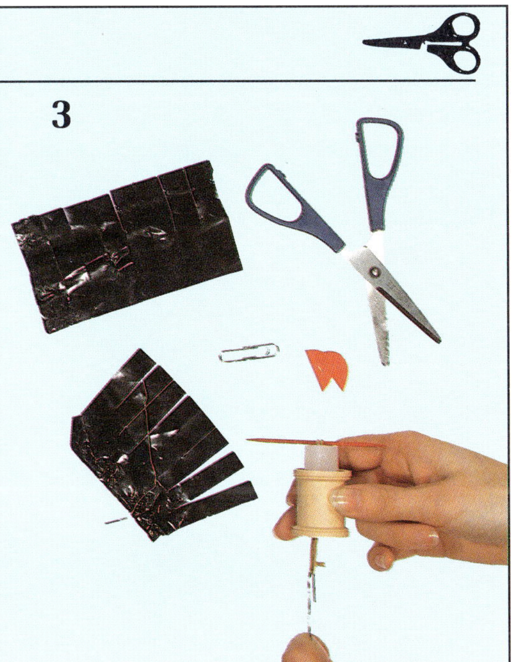

6

Bend the crawler's fringes around the generator.
6 Draw pupils on the crawler's eyes and tape them to one of the fringes.

To wind up the crawler's generator, hold the candle and toothpicks firmly in one hand and turn the cotton spool with the other hand. Give the spool a number of turns. Put the crawler down on a flat surface and watch it as it creeps along.

The crawler's toothpick should lift the creature up over objects placed in its path.

Make a different species of alien by using tinfoil instead of a trash can liner to make the body.

Pop-up Moonscape

Surprise your friends with this cratered moonscape, apparently devoid of life. Place the box on a flat surface, and watch three aliens shoot from the craters!

Step By Step

1

2

4

5

1 The bodies of the two thin aliens are drinking straws threaded onto garden stakes. The stakes must be at least 4 in longer than the height of the box used for the moonscape. Stick on modelling clay balls for eyes. The hair is tinfoil strips and tissue paper fringed with scissors pushed into the straws. **2** For the body of the larger alien, pierce a hole in an egg carton segment and thread it onto a stake. Tape a second segment to the first for an open mouth. Tape on paper teeth and tinfoil sunglasses. Fringe strips of tissue paper for the body and hair. Cut a forked paper tongue.

YOU CAN USE:

3

3 The moonscape is a large cardboard box. Cut two rings of toilet paper tube for the smaller craters. Cut a plastic bottle ring for the large crater. Cut flaps in the three craters (see page 28). Position them on top of the box. Draw around the insides of the craters and cut holes. **4** Attach the craters to the box with papier mâché – strips of newspaper dipped in a thick paste of flour and a little water. Leave it to dry. **5** Tape an extra sheet of cardboard inside the middle of the box. Make holes in the middle layer and the bottom of the box below the craters. Thread the stakes through the holes. Tape the box shut.

Decorate the aliens and moonscape with tinfoil or bright poster paint.

Practical Tips

Below are a few practical hints to help you with some of the projects described in this book and with your model-making in general.

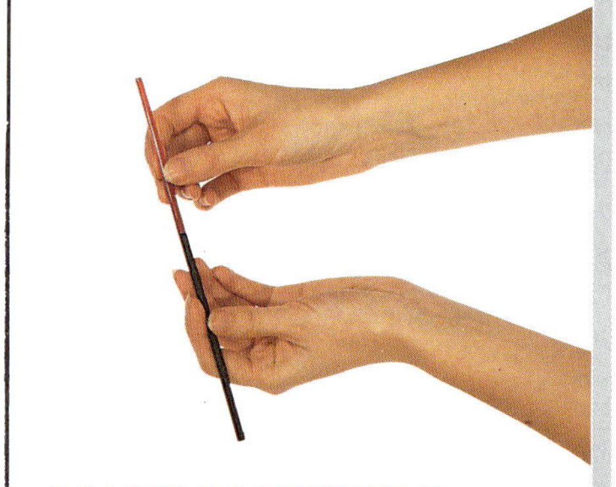

MAKING WHEELS

This tip will help you with all models that run on wheels, such as the moonbug on pages 20-1.

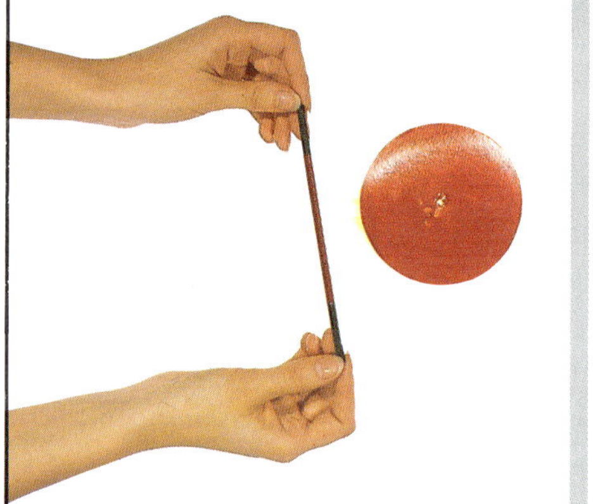

Whether your wheels are made of cardboard or plastic, they will need a cross strut or axle on which they ca[illegible] freely. A st[illegible]d through a drink[illegible] makes a good axle. If you want your model to bounce along, as the moonbug does, pierce holes for the axle off-center of your wheels.

Push the wheels onto the axle. Wind a little tape around the stake outside the wheel to secure it.

CREATING FLAPS

Use this tip for the projects on pages 8-9, 16-17, 22-23, and 26-7, and for fastening tube shapes on your models in general.

Cut a number of short slits around one end of the tube with scissors. The slits create a series of flaps. Bend

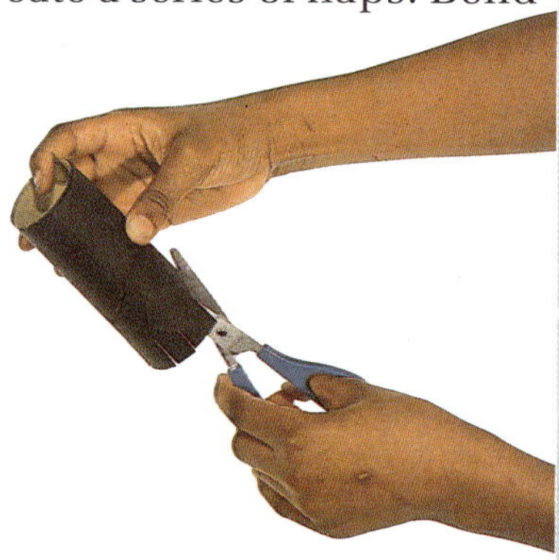

the flaps outward. Now you will be able to press the tube flat onto the surface of your model. Attach the tube to the model with glue, tape or papier mâché.

PAINTING

Poster paint, diluted with water, has been used to decorate many of the projects in this book.

To get paint to stick to plastic or tape, you could add a little dishwashing liquid to your mixing water. Stir it round with your brush or with a stick to mix it well before you begin.

NATURAL MATERIALS: twigs, leaves, petals, acorns, chestnuts, nuts, pinecones, bark, shells, pebbles, sponge, cork, feathers.

More Junk Ideas

The materials used most often in this book have been paper, cardboard and plastic packaging. Below are some more suggestions about the kinds of junk that can be used to make and decorate your models.

PAPER: newspapers, comics and magazines, postcards and birthday cards, unused wallpaper, tissue.

WOOD: garden stakes, clothespegs, cotton spools, lolly sticks.

PLASTIC: food containers, sweet and crisp wrappers, buttons, broken toys.

FABRIC: wool, socks [illegible] clothes or sheets, cloth, and felt scraps.

METAL: soft drink cans, tin foil, springs, pipecleaners, coathangers, paper clips.

Patterns

These patterns are for you to trace to help you with some of the models made in this book. You can create your own patterns very easily.

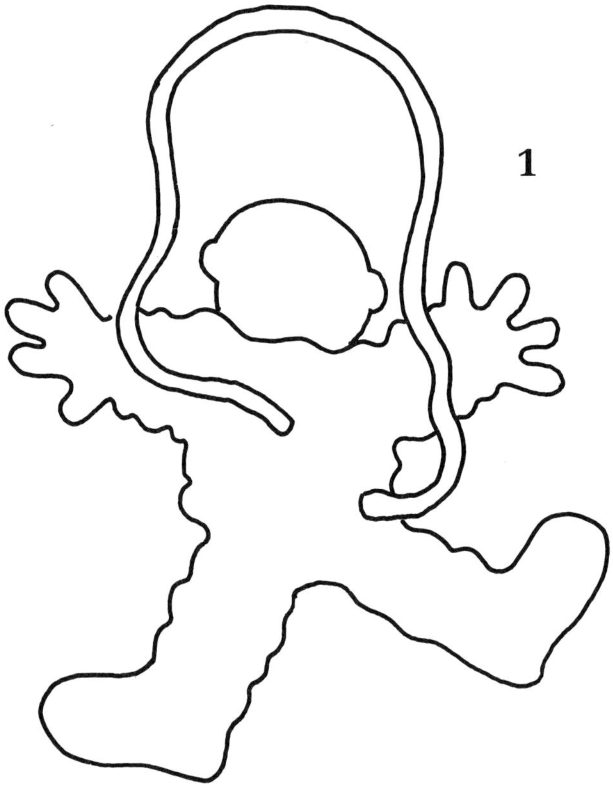

1

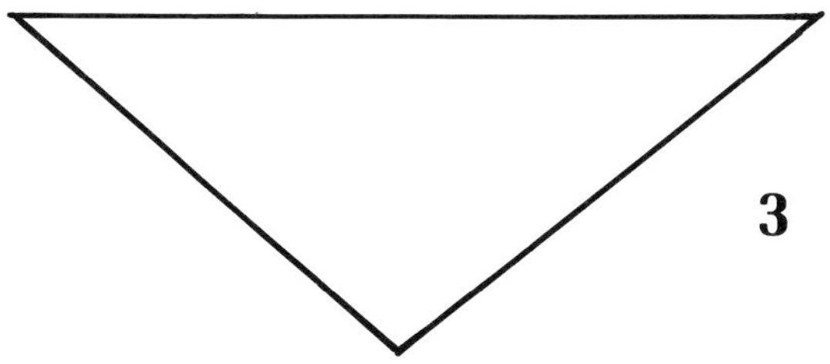

3

Use these patterns to make the space voyager mobile on pages 18-19.

1,2 Astronaut
3,4 Rocket and tailfin
5,6 Crescent moon and star

2

To use these patterns:
1 Trace the pattern shape onto tracing paper or thin bond paper.
2 Turn the tracing over, and place it on top of the paper or cardboard on which you want the image to appear. Scribble over the lines showing through the paper with your pencil. A mirror image of the pattern will appear on the cardboard.

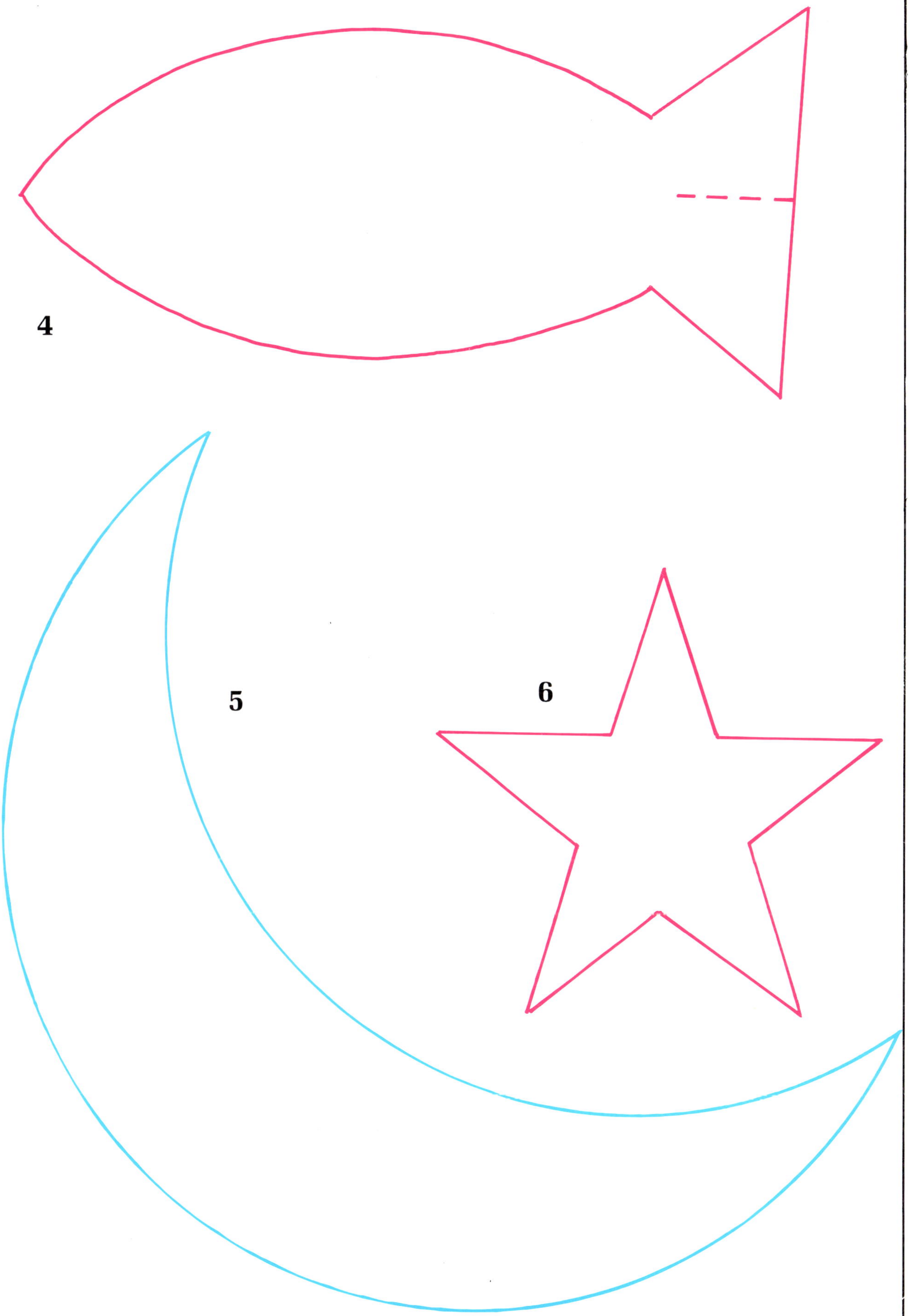
4
5
6

INDEX